Algernon Charles Swinburne

Studies in Song

Algernon Charles Swinburne

Studies in Song

ISBN/EAN: 9783742849007

Manufactured in Europe, USA, Canada, Australia, Japa

Cover: Foto ©Andreas Hilbeck / pixelio.de

Manufactured and distributed by brebook publishing software (www.brebook.com)

Algernon Charles Swinburne

Studies in Song

BY

ALGERNON CHARLES SWINBURNE

London
CHATTO & WINDUS, PICCADILLY
1880

CONTENTS.

	PAGE
SONG FOR THE CENTENARY OF WALTER SAVAGE LANDOR	1
GRAND CHORUS OF BIRDS FROM ARISTOPHANES	67
OFF SHORE	75
AFTER NINE YEARS	95
FOR A PORTRAIT OF FELICE ORSINI	103
EVENING ON THE BROADS	107
THE EMPEROR'S PROGRESS	125
THE RESURRECTION OF ALCILIA	131
THE FOURTEENTH OF JULY	135
THE LAUNCH OF THE LIVADIA	139
SIX YEARS OLD	145
A PARTING SONG	151
BY THE NORTH SEA	161

SONG FOR THE CENTENARY

OF

WALTER SAVAGE LANDOR

Born January 30th, 1775

Died September 17th, 1864

There is delight in singing, though none hear
Beside the singer: and there is delight
In praising, though the praiser sit alone
And see the praised far off him, far above.
                                        LANDOR.

DEDICATION.

TO MRS. LYNN LINTON.

Daughter in spirit elect and consecrate
  By love and reverence of the Olympian sire
Whom I too loved and worshipped, seeing so great,
  And found so gracious toward my long desire
To bid that love in song before his gate
  Sound, and my lute be loyal to his lyre,
To none save one it now may dedicate
  Song's new burnt-offering on a century's pyre.
    And though the gift be light
    As ashes in men's sight,
Left by the flame of no ethereal fire,
    Yet, for his worthier sake
    Than words are worthless, take
This wreath of words ere yet their hour expire:
    So, haply, from some heaven above,
He, seeing, may set next yours my sacrifice of love.

May 24, 1880.

SONG FOR THE CENTENARY OF WALTER SAVAGE LANDOR.

I.

FIVE years beyond an hundred years have seen
    Their winters, white as faith's and age's hue,
Melt, smiling through brief tears that broke between,
    And hope's young conquering colours reared anew,.
Since, on the day whose edge for kings made keen
    Smote sharper once than ever storm-wind blew,
A head predestined for the girdling green
    That laughs at lightning all the seasons through,.
        Nor frost or change can sunder
        Its crown untouched of thunder

Leaf from least leaf of all its leaves that grew
    Alone for brows too bold
    For storm to sear of old,
Elect to shine in time's eternal view,
    Rose on the verge of radiant life
Between the winds and sunbeams mingling love with strife.

2.

The darkling day that gave its bloodred birth
    To Milton's white republic undefiled
That might endure so few fleet years on earth
    Bore in him likewise as divine a child;
But born not less for crowns of love and mirth,
    Of palm and myrtle passionate and mild,
The leaf that girds about with gentler girth
    The brow steel-bound in battle, and the wild

Soft spray that flowers above

The flower-soft hair of love ;

And the white lips of wayworn winter smiled

And grew serene as spring's

When with stretched clouds like wings

Or wings like drift of snow-clouds massed and piled

The godlike giant, softening, spread

A shadow of stormy shelter round the new-born head.

3.

And o'er it brightening bowed the wild-haired hour,

And touched his tongue with honey and with fire,

And breathed between his lips the note of power

That makes of all the winds of heaven a lyre

Whose strings are stretched from topmost peaks that tower

To softest springs of waters that suspire,
With sounds too dim to shake the lowliest flower
  Breathless with hope and dauntless with desire :
    And bright before his face
    That Hour became a Grace,
As in the light of their Athenian quire
    When the Hours before the sun
    And Graces were made one,
Called by sweet Love down from the aerial gyre
  By one dear name of natural joy,
To bear on her bright breast from heaven a heaven-born boy.

4.

Ere light could kiss the little lids in sunder
  Or love could lift them for the sun to smite,
His fiery birth-star as a sign of wonder
  Had risen, perplexing the presageful night

WALTER SAVAGE LANDOR.

With shadow and glory around her sphere and under
   And portents prophesying by sound and sight ;
And half the sound was song and half was thunder,
   And half his life of lightning, half of light :
      And in the soft clenched hand
      Shone like a burning brand
A shadowy sword for swordless fields of fight,
      Wrought only for such lord
      As so may wield the sword
That all things ill be put to fear and flight
   Even at the flash and sweep and gleam
Of one swift stroke beheld but in a shuddering dream.

5.

Like the sun's rays that blind the night's wild beasts
   The sword of song shines as the swordsman sings ;

From the west wind's verge even to the arduous east's
    The splendour of the shadow that it flings
Makes fire and storm in heaven above the feasts
    Of men fulfilled with food of evil things;
Strikes dumb the lying and hungering lips of priests,
    Smites dead the slaying and ravening hands of kings;
        Turns dark the lamp's hot light,
        And turns the darkness bright
As with the shadow of dawn's reverberate wings;
        And far before its way
        Heaven, yearning toward the day,
Shines with its thunder and round its lightning rings;
    And never hand yet earlier played
With that keen sword whose hilt is cloud, and fire its
        blade.

6.

As dropping flakes of honey-heavy dew
    More soft than slumber's, fell the first note's sound
From strings the swift young hand strayed lightlier through
    Than leaves through calm air wheeling toward the ground
Stray down the drifting wind when skies are blue
    Nor yet the wings of latter winds unbound,
Ere winter loosen all the Æolian crew
    With storm unleashed behind them like a hound.
        As lightly rose and sank
        Beside a green-flowered bank
The clear first notes his burning boyhood found
        To sing her sacred praise
        Who rode her city's ways
Clothed with bright hair and with high purpose crowned;

A song of soft presageful breath,
Prefiguring all his love and faith in life and death ;

7.

Who should love two things only and only praise
    More than all else for ever : even the glory
Of goodly beauty in women, whence all days
    Take light whereby death's self seems transitory ;
And loftier love than loveliest eyes can raise,
    Love that wipes off the miry stains and gory
From Time's worn feet, besmirched on bloodred ways,
    And lightens with his light the night of story ;
        Love that lifts up from dust
        Life, and makes darkness just,
    And purges as with fire of purgatory

The dense disastrous air,

  To burn old falsehood bare

And give the wind its ashes heaped and hoary;

  Love, that with eyes of ageless youth

Sees on the breast of Freedom borne her nursling Truth.

8.

For at his birth the sistering stars were one

  That flamed upon it as one fiery star;

Freedom, whose light makes pale the mounting sun,

  And Song, whose fires are quenched when Freedom's

    are.

Of all that love not liberty let none

  Love her that fills our lips with fire from far

To mix with winds and seas in unison

  And sound athwart life's tideless harbour-bar

Out where our songs fly free

Across time's bounded sea,

A boundless flight beyond the dim sun's car,

Till all the spheres of night

Chime concord round their flight

Too loud for blasts of warring change to mar,

From stars that sang for Homer's birth

To these that gave our Landor welcome back from earth

9.

Shine, as above his cradle, on his grave,

Stars of our worship, lights of our desire !

For never man that heard the world's wind rave

To you was truer in trust of heart and lyre :

Nor Greece nor England on a brow more brave

Beheld your flame against the wind burn higher :

Nor all the gusts that blanch life's worldly wave
    With surf and surge could quench its flawless fire:
        No blast of all that blow
        Might bid the torch burn low
    That lightens on us yet as o'er his pyre,
        Indomitable of storm,
        That now no flaws deform
Nor thwart winds baffle ere it all aspire,
    One light of godlike breath and flame,
To write on heaven with man's most glorious names his name.

10.

The very dawn was dashed with stormy dew
    And freaked with fire as when God's hand would mar
Palaces reared of tyrants, and the blue
    Deep heaven was kindled round her thunderous car,

That saw how swift a gathering glory grew

 About him risen, ere clouds could blind or bar

A splendour strong to burn and burst them through

 And mix in one sheer light things near and far.

  First flew before his path

  Light shafts of love and wrath, .

But winged and edged as elder warriors' are;

  Then rose a light that showed

  Across the midsea road

From radiant Calpe to revealed Masar

  The way of war and love and fate

Between the goals of fear and fortune, hope and hate.

II.

Mine own twice banished fathers' harbour-land,

 Their nursing-mother France, the well-beloved,

By the arduous blast of sanguine sunrise fanned,

    Flamed on him, and his burning lips were moved

As that live statue's throned on Lybian sand

    When morning moves it, ere her light faith roved

From promise, and her tyrant's poisonous hand

    Fed hope with Corsic honey till she proved

        More deadly than despair

        And falser even than fair,

Though fairer than all elder hopes removed

        As landmarks by the crime

        Of inundating time;

Light faith by grief too loud too long reproved:

    For even as in some darkling dance

Wronged love changed hands with hate, and turned his

    heart from France.

12.

But past the snows and summits Pyrenean
  Love stronger-winged held more prevailing flight
That o'er Tyrrhene, Iberian, and Ægean
  Shores lightened with one storm of sound and light.
From earliest even to hoariest years one pæan
  Rang rapture through the fluctuant roar of fight,
From Nestor's tongue in accents Achillean
  On death's blind verge dominant over night.
    For voice as hand and hand
    As voice for one fair land
  Rose radiant, smote sonorous, past the height
    Where darkling pines enrobe
    The steel-cold Lake of Gaube,
Deep as dark death and keen as death to smite,

To where on peak or moor or plain
His heart and song and sword were one to strike for
Spain.

13.

Resurgent at his lifted voice and hand
    Pale in the light of war or treacherous fate
Song bade before him all their shadows stand
    For whom his will unbarred their funeral grate.
The father by whose wrong revenged his land
    Was given for sword and fire to desolate
Rose fire-encircled as a burning brand,
    Great as the woes he wrought and bore were great.
        Fair as she smiled and died,
        Death's crowned and breathless bride
Smiled as one living even on craft and hate:

  And pity, a star unrisen,
  Scarce lit Ferrante's prison
Ere night unnatural closed the natural gate
  That gave their life and love and light
To those fair eyes despoiled by fratricide of sight.

14.

Tears bright and sweet as fire and incense fell
  In perfect notes of music-measured pain
On veiled sweet heads that heard not love's farewell
  Sob through the song that bade them rise again ;
Rise in the light of living song, to dwell
  With memories crowned of memory : so the strain
Made soft as heaven the stream that girdles hell
  And sweet the darkness of the breathless plain,
    And with Elysian flowers

  Recrowned the wreathless hours
 That mused and mourned upon their works in vain;
  For all their works of death
  Song filled with light and breath,
 And listening grief relaxed her lightening chain;
  For sweet as all the wide sweet south
She found the song like honey from the lion's mouth.

15.

High from his throne in heaven Simonides,
 Crowned with mild aureole of memorial tears
That the everlasting sun of all time sees
 All golden, molten from the forge of years,
Smiled, as the gift was laid upon his knees
 Of songs that hang like pearls in mourners' ears,
Mild as the murmuring of Hymettian bees

And honied as their harvest, that endears

 The toil of flowery days ;

 And smiling perfect praise

Hailed his one brother mateless else of peers :

 Whom we that hear not him

 For length of date grown dim

Hear, and the heart grows glad of grief that hears;

 And harshest heights of sorrowing hours,

Like snows of Alpine April, melt from tears to flowers.

16.

Therefore to him the shadow of death was none,

 The darkness was not, nor the temporal tomb :

And multitudinous time for him was one,

 Who bade before his equal seat of doom

Rise and stand up for judgment in the sun

The weavers of the world's large-historied loom,

By their own works of light or darkness done

   Clothed round with light or girt about with gloom.

      In speech of purer gold

      Than even they spake of old

He bade the breath of Sidney's lips relume

      The fire of thought and love

      That made his bright life move

Through fair brief seasons of benignant bloom

   To blameless music ever, strong

As death and sweet as death-annihilating song.

17.

Thought gave his wings the width of time to roam,

   Love gave his thought strength equal to release

From bonds of old forgetful years, like foam

Vanished, the fame of memories that decrease ;
So strongly faith had fledged for flight from home
    The soul's large pinions till her strife should cease :
And through the trumpet of a child of Rome
    Rang the pure music of the flutes of Greece.
        As though some northern hand
        Reft from the Latin land
    A spoil more costly than the Colchian fleece
        To clothe with golden sound
        Of old joy newly found
    And rapture as of penetrating peace
        The naked north-wind's cloudiest clime,
And give its darkness light of the old Sicilian time.

18.

He saw the brand that fired the towers of Troy
    Fade, and the darkness at Œnone's prayer

Close upon her that closed upon her boy,
    For all the curse of godhead that she bare;
And the Apollonian serpent gleam and toy
    With scathless maiden limbs and shuddering hair;
And his love smitten in their dawn of joy
    Leave Pan the pine-leaf of her change to wear;
        And one in flowery coils
        Caught as in fiery toils
    Smite Calydon with mourning unaware;
        And where her low turf shrine
        Showed Modesty divine
    The fairest mother's daughter far more fair
    Hide on her breast the heavenly shame
That kindled once with love should kindle Troy with
    flame.

19.

Nor less the light of story than of song
   With graver glories girt his godlike head,
Reverted alway from the temporal throng
   Of lives that live not toward the living dead.
The shadows and the splendours of their throng
   Made bright and dark about his board and bed
The lines of life and vision, sweet or strong
   With sound of lutes or trumpets blown, that led
      Forth of the ghostly gate
      Opening in spite of fate
   Shapes of majestic or tumultuous tread,
      Divine and direful things,
      These foul as priests or kings,
Those fair as heaven or love or freedom, red

With blood and green with palms and white
With raiment woven of deeds divine and words of light.

20.

The thunder-fire of Cromwell, and the ray
   That keeps the place of Phocion's name serene
And clears the cloud from Kosciusko's day,
   Alternate as dark hours with bright between,
Met in the heaven of his high thought, which lay
   For all stars open that all eyes had seen
Rise on the night or twilight of the way
   Where feet of human hopes and fears had been.
      Again the sovereign word
      On Milton's lips was heard
   Living : again the tender three days' queen

Drew bright and gentle breath
On the sharp edge of death :
And, staged again to show of mortal scene,
Tiberius, ere his name grew dire,
Wept, stainless yet of empire, tears of blood and fire.

21.

Most ardent and most awful and most fond,
The fervour of his Apollonian eye
Yearned upon Hellas, yet enthralled in bond
Of time whose years beheld her and past by
Silent and shameful, till she rose and donned
The casque again of Pallas ; for her cry
Forth of the past and future, depths beyond
This where the present and its tyrants lie,
As one great voice of twain

    For him had pealed again,
Heard but of hearts high as her own was high,
      High as her own and his
      And pure as love's heart is,
That lives though hope at once and memory die :
    And with her breath his clarion's blast
Was filled as cloud with fire or future souls with past.

22.

As a wave only obsequious to the wind
    Leaps to the lifting breeze that bids it leap,
Large-hearted, and its thickening mane be thinned
    By the strong god's breath moving on the deep
From utmost Atlas even to extremest Ind
    That shakes the plain where no men sow nor reap,
So, moved with wrath toward men that ruled and sinned

And pity toward all tears he saw men weep,
    Arose to take man's part
    His loving lion heart,
Kind as the sun's that has in charge to keep
    Earth and the seed thereof
    Safe in his lordly love,
Strong as sheer truth and soft as very sleep ;
    The mightiest heart since Milton's leapt,
The gentlest since the gentlest heart of Shakespeare
    slept.

23.

Like the wind's own on her divided sea
    His song arose on Corinth, and aloud
Recalled her Isthmian song and strife when she
    Was thronged with glories as with gods in crowd

And as the wind's own spirit her breath was free
    And as the heaven's own heart her soul was proud,
But freer and prouder stood no son than he
    Of all she bare before her heart was bowed;
        None higher than he who heard
        Medea's keen last word
Transpierce her traitor, and like a rushing cloud
        That sundering shows a star
        Saw pass her thunderous car
And a face whiter and deadlier than a shroud
    That lightened from it, and the brand
Of tender blood that falling seared his suppliant hand.

24.

More fair than all things born and slain of fate,
    More glorious than all births of days and nights,

He bade the spirit of man regenerate,
   Rekindling, rise and reassume the rights
That in high seasons of his old estate
   Clothed him and armed with majesties and mights
Heroic, when the times and hearts were great
   And in the depths of ages rose the heights
      Radiant of high deeds done
      And souls that matched the sun
For splendour with the lightnings of their lights
      Whence even their uttered names
      Burn like the strong twin flames
Of song that shakes a throne and steel that smites ;
   As on Thermopylæ when shone
Leonidas, on Syracuse Timoleon.

25.

Or, sweeter than the breathless buds when spring
    With smiles and tears and kisses bids them breathe,
Fell with its music from his quiring string
    Fragrance of pine-leaves and odorous heath
Twined round the lute whereto he sighed to sing
    Of the oak that screened and showed its maid beneath,
Who seeing her bee crawl back with broken wing
    Faded, a fairer flower than all her wreath,
        And paler, though her oak
        Stood scathless of the stroke
    More sharp than edge of axe or wolfish teeth,
        That mixed with mortals dead
        Her own half heavenly head
And life incorporate with a sylvan sheath,
    And left the wild rose and the dove
A secret place and sacred from all guests but Love.

26.

But in the sweet clear fields beyond the river
  Dividing pain from peace and man from shade
He saw the wings that there no longer quiver
  Sink of the hours whose parting footfalls fade
On ears which hear the rustling amaranth shiver
  With sweeter sound of wind than ever made
Music on earth : departing, they deliver
  The soul that shame or wrath or sorrow swayed ;
    And round the king of men
    Clash the clear arms again,
  Clear of all soil and bright as laurel braid,
    That rang less high for joy
    Through the gates fallen of Troy
Than here to hail the sacrificial maid,

Iphigeneia, when the ford

Fast-flowing of sorrows brought her father and their lord.

27.

And in the clear gulf of the hollow sea
    He saw light glimmering through the grave green gloom
That hardly gave the sun's eye leave to see
    Cymodameia ; but nor tower nor tomb,
No tower on earth, no tomb of waves may be,
    That may not sometime by diviner doom
Be plain and pervious to the poet ; he
    Bids time stand back from him and fate make room
        For passage of his feet,
        Strong as their own are fleet,
And yield the prey no years may reassume

Through all their clamorous track,

Nor night nor day win back

Nor give to darkness what his eyes illume

And his lips bless for ever : he

Knows what earth knows not, sings truth sung not of the

sea.

28.

Before the sentence of a curule chair

More sacred than the Roman, rose and stood

To take their several doom the imperial pair

Diversely born of Venus, and in mood

Diverse as their one mother, and as fair,

Though like two stars contrasted, and as good,

Though different as dark eyes from golden hair ;

One as that iron planet red like blood

That bears among the stars

Fierce witness of her Mars

In bitter fire by her sweet light subdued;
    One in the gentler skies
    Sweet as her amorous eyes:
One proud of worlds and seas and darkness rude
    Composed and conquered; one content
With lightnings from loved eyes of lovers lightly sent.

29.

And where Alpheus and where Ladon ran
    Radiant, by many a rushy and rippling cove
More known to glance of god than wandering man,
    He sang the strife of strengths divine that strove,
Unequal, one with other, for a span,
    Who should be friends for ever in heaven above
And here on pastoral earth: Arcadian Pan,

And the awless lord of kings and shepherds, Love :
　　All the sweet strife and strange
　　With fervid counterchange
Till one fierce wail through many a glade and grove
　　Rang, and its breath made shiver
　　The reeds of many a river,
And the warm airs waxed wintry that it clove,
　　Keen-edged as ice-retempered brand ;
Nor might god's hurt find healing save of godlike hand.

30.

As when the jarring gates of thunder ope
　　Like earthquake felt in heaven, so dire a cry,
So fearful and so fierce—'Give the sword scope !'—
　　Rang from a daughter's lips, darkening the sky

To the extreme azure of all its cloudless cope
    With starless horror : nor the God's own eye
Whose doom bade smite, whose ordinance bade hope,
    Might well endure to see the adulteress die,
        The husband-slayer fordone
        By swordstroke of her son,
Unutterable, unimaginable on high,
        On earth abhorrent, fell
        Beyond all scourge of hell,
Yet righteous as redemption : Love stood nigh,
    Mute, sister-like, and closer clung
Than all fierce forms of threatening coil and maddening
    tongue.

31.

All these things heard and seen and sung of old,
    He heard and saw and sang them. Once again

Might foot of man tread, eye of man behold
    Things unbeholden save of ancient men,
Ways save by gods untrodden. In his hold
    The staff that stayed through some Ætnean glen
The steps of the most highest, most awful-souled
    And mightiest-mouthed of singers, even as then
        Became a prophet's rod,
        A lyre on fire of God,
Being still the staff of exile : yea, as when
        The voice poured forth on us
        Was even of Æschylus,
And his one word great as the crying of ten,
    Crying in men's ears of wrath toward wrong,
Of love toward right immortal, sanctified with song.

32.

Him too whom none save one before him ever
    Beheld, nor since hath man again beholden,
Whom Dante seeing him saw not, nor the giver
    Of all gifts back to man by time withholden,
Shakespeare—him too, whom sea-like ages sever,
    As waves divide men's eyes from lights upholden
To landward, from our songs that find him never,
    Seeking, though memory fire and hope embolden—
        Him too this one song found,
        And raised at its sole sound
Up from the dust of darkling dreams and olden
        Legends forlorn of breath,
        Up from the deeps of death,
Ulysses: him whose name turns all songs golden,
    The wise divine strong soul, whom fate
Could make no less than change and chance beheld him
    great.

33.

Nor stands the seer who raised him less august
  Before us, nor in judgment frail and rathe,
Less constant or less loving or less just,
  But fruitful-ripe and full of tender faith,
Holding all high and gentle names in trust
  Of time for honour ; so his quickening breath
Called from the darkness of their martyred dust
  Our sweet Saints Alice and Elizabeth,
    Revived and reinspired
    With speech from heavenward fired
By love to say what Love the Archangel saith
    Only, nor may such word
    Save by such ears be heard
As hear the tongues of angels after death

Descending on them like a dove

Has taken all earthly sense of thought away but love.

34.

All sweet, all sacred, all heroic things,

    All generous names and loyal, and all wise,

With all his heart in all its wayfarings

    He sought, and worshipped, seeing them with his eyes

In very present glory, clothed with wings

    Of words and deeds and dreams immortal, rise

Visible more than living slaves and kings,

    Audible more than actual vows and lies :

        These, with scorn's fieriest rod,

        These and the Lord their God,

    The Lord their likeness, tyrant of the skies

As they Lord Gods of earth,

These with a rage of mirth

He mocked and scourged and spat on, in such wise

That none might stand before his rod,

And these being slain the Spirit alone be lord or God.

35.

For of all souls for all time glorious none

    Loved Freedom better, of all who have loved her best,

Than he who wrote that scripture of the sun

    Writ as with fire and light on heaven's own crest,

Of all words heard on earth the noblest one

    That ever spake for souls and left them blest:

GLADLY WE SHOULD REST EVER, HAD WE WON

    FREEDOM: WE HAVE LOST, AND VERY GLADLY REST.

O poet hero, lord
And father, we record
Deep in the burning tablets of the breast
Thankfully those divine
And living words of thine
For faith and comfort in our hearts imprest
With strokes engraven past hurt of years
And lines inured with fire of immemorial tears.

36.

But who being less than thou shall sing of thee
Words worthy of more than pity or less than scorn?
Who sing the golden garland woven of three,
Thy daughters, Graces mightier than the morn,
More godlike than the graven gods men see
Made all but all immortal, human born

And heavenly natured? With the first came He,
  Led by the living hand, who left forlorn
    Life by his death, and time
    More by his life sublime
  Than by the lives of all whom all men mourn,
    And even for mourning praise
    Heaven, as for all those days
  These dead men's lives clothed round with glories worn
  By memory till all time lie dead,
And higher than all behold the bay round Shakespeare's head.

37.

Then, fairer than the fairest Grace of ours,
  Came girt with Grecian gold the second Grace,

And verier daughter of his most perfect hours
    Than any of latter time or alien place
Named, or with hair inwoven of English flowers
    Only, nor wearing on her statelier face
The lordlier light of Athens.   All the Powers
    That graced and guarded round that holiest race,
        That heavenliest and most high
        Time hath seen live and die,
Poured all their power upon him to retrace
        The erased immortal roll
        Of Love's most sovereign scroll
And Wisdom's warm from Freedom's wide embrace,
    The scroll that on Aspasia's knees
Laid once made manifest the Olympian Pericles.

38.

Clothed on with tenderest weft of Tuscan air,
 Came laughing like Etrurian spring the third,
With green Valdelsa's hill-flowers in her hair
 Deep-drenched with May-dews, in her voice the bird
Whose voice hath night and morning in it ; fair
 As the ambient gold of wall-flowers that engird
The walls engirdling with a circling stair
 My sweet San Gimignano : nor a word
  Fell from her flowerlike mouth
  Not sweet with all the south ;
As though the dust shrined in Certaldo stirred
  And spake, as o'er it shone
  That bright Pentameron,
And his own vines again and chestnuts heard
 Boccaccio : nor swift Elsa's chime
Mixed not her golden babble with Petrarca's rhyme.

39.

No lovelier laughed the garden which receives
    Yet, and yet hides not from our following eyes
With soft rose-laurels and low strawberry-leaves,
    Ternissa, sweet as April-coloured skies,
Bowed like a flowering reed when May's wind heaves
    The reed-bed that the stream kisses and sighs,
In love that shrinks and murmurs and believes
    What yet the wisest of the starriest wise
        Whom Greece might ever hear
        Speaks in the gentlest ear
That ever heard love's lips philosophize
        With such deep-reasoning words
        As blossoms use and birds,
Nor heeds Leontion lingering till they rise

    Far off, in no wise over far,
Beneath a heaven all amorous of its first-born star.

40.

What sound, what storm and splendour of what fire,
　　Darkening the light of heaven, lightening the night,
Rings, rages, flashes round what ravening pyre
　　That makes time's face pale with its reflex light
And leaves on earth, who seeing might scarce respire,
　　A shadow of red remembrance? Right nor might
Alternating wore ever shapes more dire
　　Nor manifest in all men's awful sight
　　　　In form and face that wore
　　　　Heaven's light and likeness more
Than these, or held suspense men's hearts at height

More fearful, since man first
    Slaked with man's blood his thirst,
Than when Rome clashed with Hannibal in fight,
    Till tower on ruining tower was hurled
Where Scipio stood, and Carthage was not in the world.

41.

Nor lacked there power of purpose in his hand
    Who carved their several praise in words of gold
To bare the brows of conquerors and to brand,
    Made shelterless of laurels bought and sold
For price of blood or incense, dust or sand,
    Triumph or terror. He that sought of old
His father Ammon in a stranger's land,
    And shrank before the serpentining fold,

Stood in our seer's wide eye

No higher than man most high,

And lowest in heart when highest in hope to hold

Fast as a scripture furled

The scroll of all the world

Sealed with his signet : nor the blind and bold

First thief of empire, round whose head

Swarmed carrion flies for bees, on flesh for violets fed.[1]

42.

As fire that kisses, killing with a kiss,

He saw the light of death, riotous and red,

Flame round the bent brows of Semiramis

Re-risen, and mightier, from the Assyrian dead,

[1] Thy lifelong works, Napoleon, who shall write?
Time, in his children's blood who takes delight.
From the Greek of Landor.

Kindling, as dawn a frost-bound precipice,

    The steely snows of Russia, for the tread

Of feet that felt before them crawl and hiss

    The snaky lines of blood violently shed.

        Like living creeping things

        That writhe but have no stings

To scare adulterers from the imperial bed

        Bowed with its load of lust,

        Or chill the ravenous gust

That made her body a fire from heel to head ;

    Or change her high bright spirit and clear,

For all its mortal stains, from taint of fraud or fear.

43.

As light that blesses, hallowing with a look;.

    He saw the godhead in Vittoria's face

Shine soft on Buonarroti's, till he took,

 Albeit himself God, a more godlike grace,

A strength more heavenly to confront and brook

 All ill things coiled about his worldly race,

From the bright scripture of that present book

 Wherein his tired grand eyes got power to trace

  Comfort more sweet than youth,

  And hope whose child was truth,

And love that brought forth sorrow for a space,

  Only that she might bear

  Joy : these things, written there,

Made even his soul's high heaven a heavenlier place,

 Perused with eyes whose glory and glow

Had in their fires the spirit of Michael Angelo.

44.

With balms and dews of blessing he consoled
   The fair fame wounded by the black priest's fang,
Giovanna's, and washed off her blithe and bold
   Boy-bridegroom's blood, that seemed so long to hang
On her fair hand, even till the stain of old
   Was cleansed with healing song, that after sang
Sharp truth by sweetest singers' lips untold
   Of pale Beatrice, though her death-note rang
      From other strings divine
      Ere his rekindling line
With yet more piteous and intolerant pang
      Pierced all men's hearts anew
      That heard her passion through
Till fierce from throes of fiery pity sprang

Wrath, armed for chase of monstrous beasts,
Strong to lay waste the kingdom of the seed of priests.

45.

He knew the high-souled humbleness, the mirth
    And majesty of meanest men born free,
That made with Luther's or with Hofer's birth
    The whole world worthier of the sun to see:
The wealth of spirit among the snows, the dearth
    Wherein souls festered by the servile sea
That saw the lowest of even crowned heads on earth
    Thronged round with worship in Parthenope.
        His hand bade Justice guide
        Her child Tyrannicide,
Light winged by fire that brings the dawn to be;

And pierced with Tyrrel's dart
     Again the riotous heart
That mocked at mercy's tongue and manhood's knee:
  And oped the cell where kinglike death
Hung o'er her brows discrowned who bare Elizabeth.

46.

Toward Spenser or toward Bacon proud or kind
   He bared the heart of Essex, twain and one,
For the base heart that soiled the starry mind
   Stern, for the father in his child undone
Soft as his own toward children, stamped and signed
   With their sweet image visibly set on
As by God's hand, clear as his own designed
   The likeness radiant out of ages gone

That none may now destroy

Of that high Roman boy

Whom Julius and Cleopatra saw their son

True-born of sovereign seed,

Foredoomed even thence to bleed,

The stately grace of bright Cæsarion,

The head unbent, the heart unbowed,

That not the shadow of death could make less clear and

proud.

47.

With gracious gods he communed, honouring thus

At once by service and similitude,

Service devout and worship emulous

Of the same golden Muses once they wooed,

The names and shades adored of all of us,

The nurslings of the brave world's earlier brood,

Grown gods for us themselves : Theocritus

    First, and more dear Catullus, names bedewed

        With blessings bright like tears

        From the old memorial years,

    And loves and lovely laughters, every mood

        Sweet as the drops that fell

        Of their own œnomel

    From living lips to cheer the multitude

        That feeds on words divine, and grows

More worthy, seeing their world reblossom like a rose.

48.

Peace, the soft seal of long life's closing story,

    The silent music that no strange note jars,

Crowned not with gentler hand the years that glory

    Crowned, but could hide not all the spiritual scars

Time writes on the inward strengths of warriors hoary
   With much long warfare, and with gradual bars
Blindly pent in : but these, being transitory,
   Broke, and the power came back that passion mars :
      And at the lovely last
      Above all anguish past
Before his own the sightless eyes like stars
      Arose that watched arise
      Like stars in other skies
   Above the strife of ships and hurtling cars
     The Dioscurian songs divine
That lighten all the world with lightning of their line.

49.

He sang the last of Homer, having sung
   The last of his Ulysses.   Bright and wide

For him time's dark strait ways, like clouds that clung
    About the day-star, doubtful to divide,
Waxed in his spiritual eyeshot, and his tongue
    Spake as his soul bore witness, that descried,
Like those twin towering lights in darkness hung,
    Homer, and grey Laertes at his side
        Kingly as kings are none
        Beneath a later sun,
    And the sweet maiden ministering in pride
        To sovereign and to sage
        In their more sweet old age:
These things he sang, himself as old, and died.
    And if death be not, if life be,
As Homer and as Milton are in heaven is he.

WALTER SAVAGE LANDOR.

50.

Poet whose large-eyed loyalty of love
   Was pure toward all high poets, all their kind
And all bright words and all sweet works thereof;
   Strong like the sun, and like the sunlight kind;
Heart that no fear but every grief might move
   Wherewith men's hearts were bound of powers that bind;
The purest soul that ever proof could prove
   From taint of tortuous or of envious mind;
     Whose eyes elate and clear
     Nor shame nor ever fear
But only pity or glorious wrath could blind;
     Name set for love apart,
     Held lifelong in my heart,
Face like a father's toward my face inclined;
   No gifts like thine are mine to give,
Who by thine own words only bid thee hail, and live.

NOTES.

6. See note to the Imaginary Conversation of Leofric and Godiva for the exquisite first verses extant from the hand of Landor.
10. The Poems of Walter Savage Landor: 1795. Moral Epistle, respectfully dedicated to Earl Stanhope: 1795. Gebir.
13. Count Julian: Ines de Castro: Ippolito di Este.
14, 15. Poems 'on the Dead.'
16. Imaginary Conversations: Lord Brooke and Sir Philip Sidney.
17, 18. Idyllia Nova Quinque Heroum atque Heroidum (1815): Corythus; Dryope; Pan et Pitys; Coresus et Callirrhoe; Helena ad Pudoris Aram.
19, 20. Imaginary Conversations: Oliver Cromwell and Walter Noble; Æschines and Phocion; Kosciusko and Poniatowski; Milton and Marvell; Roger Ascham and Lady Jane Grey; Tiberius and Vipsania.
21, 22, 23. Hellenics: To Corinth.
24. Hellenics: Regeneration.
25. The Hamadryad; Acon and Rhodope.
26. The Shades of Agamemnon and Iphigeneia.

STANZA

27. Enallos and Cymodameia.

28. The Children of Venus.

29. Cupid and Pan.

30. The Death of Clytemnestra; The Madness of Orestes; The Prayer of Orestes.

32. The Last of Ulysses.

33. Imaginary Conversations. Lady Lisle and Elizabeth Gaunt.

35. *Pro monumento super milites regio jussu interemptos.*

36. The Citation and Examination of William Shakespeare.

37. Pericles and Aspasia.

38. The Pentameron.

39. Imaginary Conversations: Epicurus, Leontion, and Ternissa.

40. Marcellus and Hannibal: P. Scipio Æmilianus, Polybius, and Panætius.

41. Alexander and Priest of Ammon: Bonaparte and the President of the Senate.

42. The Empress Catherine and Princess Dashkoff.

43. Vittoria Colonna and Michel-Angelo Buonarroti.

44. Andrea of Hungary, Giovanna of Naples, Fra Rupert; a Trilogy: Five Scenes (Beatrice Cenci).

45. Luther's Parents: The Death of Hofer: (*Imaginary Conversations*) Andrew Hofer, Count Metternich, and the Emperor Francis; Judge Wolfgang and Henry of Melchthal: The Coronation. Tyrannicide (*The Last Fruit off an Old Tree*): Walter Tyrrel and William Rufus: Henry VIII. and Anne Boleyn.

STANZA
46. Essex and Spenser (*Imaginary Conversations*): Essex and Bacon: Antony and Octavius (*Scenes for the Study*).

47. Critical Essays on Theocritus and Catullus.

48, 49. Heroic Idyls: Homer, Laertes, and Agatha.

'J'en passe, et des meilleurs.' But who can enumerate all or half our obligations to the illimitable and inexhaustible genius of the great man whose life and whose labour lasted even from the generation of our fathers' fathers to our own? Hardly any reader can feel, I think, so deeply as I feel the inadequacy of my poor praise and too imperfect gratitude to the majestic subject of their attempted expression; but 'such as I had have I given him.'

GRAND CHORUS OF BIRDS

FROM

ARISTOPHANES

Attempted in English verse after the original metre.

I WAS allured into the audacity of this experiment by consideration of a fact which hitherto does not seem to have been taken into consideration by any translator of the half divine humourist in whose incomparable genius the highest qualities of Rabelais were fused and harmonized with the supremest gifts of Shelley: namely, that his marvellous metrical invention of the anapæstic heptameter was almost exactly reproducible in a language to which all variations and combinations of anapæstic, iambic, or trochaic metre are as natural and pliable as all dactylic and spondaic forms of verse are unnatural and abhorrent. As it happens, this highest central interlude of a most adorable masterpiece is as easy to detach from its dramatic setting, and even from its lyrical context, as it was easy to give line for line of it in English. In two metrical points only does my version vary from the verbal pattern of the original. I have of course added rhymes, and double rhymes, as necessary makeweights for the imperfection of an otherwise inadequate language; and equally of course I have not attempted the impossible and undesirable task of reproducing the rare exceptional effect of a line overcharged on purpose with a preponderance of heavy-footed spondees: and this for the obvious reason that even if such a line—which I doubt—could be exactly represented, foot by foot and pause for pause, in English, this English line would no more be a verse in any proper sense of the word than is the line I am writing at this moment. And my main intention, or at least my main desire, in the undertaking of this brief adventure, was to renew as far as possible for English ears the music of this resonant and triumphant metre, which goes ringing at full gallop as of horses who

> 'dance as 'twere to the music
> Their own hoofs make.'

I would not seem over curious in search of an apt or inapt quotation: but nothing can be fitter than a verse of Shakespeare's to praise at once and to describe the most typical verse of Aristophanes.

THE BIRDS.

(685-723.)

COME on then, ye dwellers by nature in darkness, and like to the leaves' generations,

That are little of might, that are moulded of mire, unenduring and shadowlike nations,

Poor plumeless ephemerals, comfortless mortals, as visions of creatures fast fleeing,

Lift up your mind unto us that are deathless, and dateless the date of our being:

Us, children of heaven, us, ageless for aye, us, all of
    whose thoughts are eternal ;
That ye may from henceforth, having heard of us all things
    aright as to matters supernal,
Of the being of birds and beginning of gods, and of
    streams, and the dark beyond reaching,
Truthfully knowing aright, in my name bid Prodicus pack
    with his preaching.

It was Chaos and Night at the first, and the blackness
    of darkness, and hell's broad border,
Earth was not, nor air, neither heaven ; when in depths
    of the womb of the dark without order
First thing first-born of the black-plumed Night was a
    wind-egg hatched in her bosom,
Whence timely with seasons revolving again sweet Love
    burst out as a blossom,

Gold wings glittering forth of his back, like whirlwinds gustily turning.

He, after his wedlock with Chaos, whose wings are of darkness, in hell broad-burning,

For his nestlings begat him the race of us first, and upraised us to light new-lighted.

And before this was not the race of the gods, until all things by Love were united;

And of kind united with kind in communion of nature the sky and the sea are

Brought forth, and the earth, and the race of the gods everlasting and blest. So that we are

Far away the most ancient of all things blest. And that we are of Love's generation

There are manifest manifold signs. We have wings, and with us have the Loves habitation;

And manifold fair young folk that forswore love once,
    ere the bloom of them ended,
Have the men that pursued and desired them subdued,
    by the help of us only befriended,
With such baits as a quail, a flamingo, a goose, or a cock's
    comb staring and splendid.

All best good things that befall men come from us
    birds, as is plain to all reason :
For first we proclaim and make known to them spring,
    and the winter and autumn in season ;
Bid sow, when the crane starts clanging for Afric, in
    shrill-voiced emigrant number,
And calls to the pilot to hang up his rudder again for the
    season, and slumber ;
And then weave a cloak for Orestes the thief, lest he
    strip men of theirs if it freezes.

And again thereafter the kite reappearing announces a
> change in the breezes,
And that here is the season for shearing your sheep of
> their spring wool.   Then does the swallow
Give you notice to sell your greatcoat, and provide some-
> thing light for the heat that's to follow.
Thus are we as Ammon or Delphi unto you, Dodona,
> nay, Phœbus Apollo.
For, as first ye come all to get auguries of birds, even such
> is in all things your carriage,
Be the matter a matter of trade, or of earning your bread,
> or of any one's marriage.
And all things ye lay to the charge of a bird that belong
> to discerning prediction :
Winged fame is a bird, as you reckon : you sneeze, and
> the sign's as a bird for conviction :

All tokens are 'birds' with you—sounds too, and lackeys,
    and donkeys. Then must it not follow
That we ARE to you all as the manifest godhead that
    speaks in prophetic Apollo?

October 19, 1880.

OFF SHORE

OFF SHORE.

When the might of the summer

 Is most on the sea ;

When the days overcome her

 With joy but to be,

With rapture of royal enchantment, and sorcery that sets

 her not free,

But for hours upon hours

 As a thrall she remains

Spell-bound as with flowers

 And content in their chains,

And her loud steeds fret not, and lift not a lock of their

 deep white manes ;

Then only, far under

    In the depths of her hold,

Some gleam of its wonder

    Man's eye may behold,

Its wild-weed forests of crimson and russet and olive and gold.

Still deeper and dimmer

    And goodlier they glow

For the eyes of the swimmer

    Who scans them below

As he crosses the zone of their flowerage that knows not of sunshine and snow.

Soft blossomless frondage

    And foliage that gleams

As to prisoners in bondage

The light of their dreams,
The desire of a dawn unbeholden, with hope on the wings of its beams.

Not as prisoners entombed
Waxen haggard and wizen,
But consoled and illumed
In the depths of their prison
With delight of the light everlasting and vision of dawn on them risen,

From the banks and the beds
. Of the waters divine
They lift up their heads
And the flowers of them shine
Through the splendour of darkness that clothes them of water that glimmers like wine.

Bright bank over bank
Making glorious the gloom,
Soft rank upon rank,
Strange bloom after bloom,
They kindle the liquid low twilight, the dusk of the dim sea's womb.

Through the subtle and tangible
Gloom without form,
Their branches, infrangible
Ever of storm
Spread softer their sprays than the shoots of the woodland when April is warm.

As the flight of the thunder, full
Charged with its word,
Dividing the wonderful

OFF SHORE.

    Depths like a bird,
Speaks wrath and delight to the heart of the night that exults to have heard,

    So swiftly, though soundless
      In silence's ear,
    Light, winged from the boundless
      Blue depths full of cheer,
Speaks joy to the heart of the waters that part not before him, but hear.

    Light, perfect and visible
      Godhead of God,
    God indivisible,
      Lifts but his rod,
And the shadows are scattered in sunder, and darkness is light at his nod.

At the touch of his wand,

    At the nod of his head

From the spaces beyond

    Where the dawn hath her bed,

Earth, water, and air are transfigured, and rise as one risen from the dead.

He puts forth his hand,

    And the mountains are thrilled

To the heart as they stand

    In his presence, fulfilled

With his glory that utters his grace upon earth, and her sorrows are stilled.

The moan of her travail

    That groans for the light

Till dayspring unravel

The weft of the night,

At the sound of the strings of the music of morning, falls

dumb with delight.

He gives forth his word,

And the word that he saith,

Ere well it be heard,

Strikes darkness to death ;

For the thought of his heart is the sunrise, and dawn as

the sound of his breath.

And the strength of its pulses

That passion makes proud

Confounds and convulses

The depths of the cloud

Of the darkness that heaven was engirt with, divided and

rent as a shroud,

As the veil of the shrine

Of the temple of old

When darkness divine

Over noonday was rolled;

So the heart of the night by the pulse of the light is con-

vulsed and controlled.

And the sea's heart, groaning

For glories withdrawn,

And the waves' mouths, moaning

All night for the dawn,

Are uplift as the hearts and the mouths of the singers on

leaside and lawn.

And the sound of the quiring

Of all these as one,

Desired and desiring

Till dawn's will be done,

Fills full with delight of them heaven till it burns as the heart of the sun.

Till the waves too inherit
And waters take part
In the sense of the spirit
That breathes from his heart,
And are kindled with music as fire when the lips of the morning part,

With music unheard
In the light of her lips,
In the life-giving word
Of the dewfall that drips
On the grasses of earth, and the wind that enkindles the wings of the ships.

White glories of wings
As of seafaring birds
That flock from the springs
Of the sunrise in herds
With the wind for a herdsman, and hasten or halt at the change of his words.

As the watchword's change
When the wind's note shifts,
And the skies grow strange,
And the white squall drifts
Up sharp from the sea-line, vexing the sea till the low cloud lifts.

At the charge of his word
Bidding pause, bidding haste,
When the ranks are stirred

And the lines displaced,
They scatter as wild swans parting adrift on the wan green waste.

At the hush of his word
In a pause of his breath
When the waters have heard
His will that he saith,
They stand as a flock penned close in its fold for division of death.

As a flock by division
Of death to be thinned,
As the shades in a vision
Of spirits that sinned ;
So glimmer their shrouds and their sheetings as clouds on the stream of the wind.

But the sun stands fast,

 And the sea burns bright,

And the flight of them past

 Is no more than the flight

Of the snow-soft swarm of serene wings poised and afloat in the light.

Like flowers upon flowers

 In a festival way

When hours after hours

 Shed grace on the day,

White blossomlike butterflies hover and gleam through the snows of the spray.

Like snow-coloured petals

 Of blossoms that flee

From storm that unsettles

The flower as the tree

They flutter, a legion of flowers on the wing, through the field of the sea.

Through the furrowless field

Where the foam-blossoms blow

And the secrets are sealed

Of their harvest below

They float in the path of the sunbeams, as flakes or as blossoms of snow.

Till the sea's ways darken,

And the God, withdrawn,

Give ear not or hearken

If prayer on him fawn,

And the sun's self seem but a shadow, the noon as a ghost of the dawn.

No shadow, but rather

God, father of song,

Shew grace to me, Father

God, loved of me long,

That I lose not the light of thy face, that my trust in thee

work me not wrong.

While yet I make forward

With face toward thee

Not turned yet in shoreward,

Be thine upon me ;

Be thy light on my forehead or ever I turn it again from

the sea.

As a kiss on my brow

Be the light of thy grace,

Be thy glance on me now

From the pride of thy place :
As the sign of a sire to a son be the light on my face of thy face.

Thou wast father of olden
    Times hailed and adored,
And the sense of thy golden
    Great harp's monochord
Was the joy in the soul of the singers that hailed thee for master and lord.

Fair father of all
    In thy ways that have trod,
That have risen at thy call,
    That have thrilled at thy nod,
Arise, shine, lighten upon me, O sun that we see to be God.

As my soul has been dutiful
 Only to thee,
O God most beautiful,
 Lighten thou me,
As I swim through the dim long rollers, with eyelids uplift from the sea.

Be praised and adored of us
 All in accord,
Father and lord of us
 Alway adored,
The slayer and the stayer and the harper, the light of us all and our lord.

At the sound of thy lyre,
 At the touch of thy rod,
Air quickens to fire

By the foot of thee trod,
The saviour and healer and singer, the living and visible God.

The years are before thee
As shadows of thee,
As men that adore thee,
As cloudlets that flee :
But thou art the God, and thy kingdom is heaven, and thy shrine is the sea.

AFTER NINE YEARS

AFTER NINE YEARS.

TO JOSEPH MAZZINI.

Primâ dicte mihi, summâ dicende Camenâ.

I.

The shadows fallen of years are nine

Since heaven grew seven times more divine

With thy soul entering, and the dearth

Of souls on earth

Grew sevenfold sadder, wanting One

Whose light of life, quenched here and done,

Burns there eternal as the sun.

2.

Beyond all word, beyond all deed,

Beyond all thought beloved, what need

Has death or love that speech should be,

Hast thou of me?

I had no word, no prayer, no cry,

To praise or hail or mourn thee by,

As when thou too wast man as I.

3.

Nay, never, nor as any born

Save one whose name priests turn to scorn,

Who haply, though we know not now,

Was man as thou,

A wanderer branded with men's blame,

Loved past man's utterance : yea, the same,

Perchance, and as his name thy name.

4.

Thou wast as very Christ—not he

Degraded into Deity,

And priest-polluted by such prayer

As poisons air,

Tongue-worship of the tongue that slays,

False faith and parricidal praise :

But the man crowned with suffering days.

5.

God only, being of all mankind

Most manlike, of most equal mind

And heart most perfect, more than can

Be heart of man

Once in ten ages, born to be

As haply Christ was, and as we

Knew surely, seeing, and worshipped thee.

6.

To know thee—this at least was ours,

God, clothed upon with human hours,

O face beloved, O spirit adored,

Saviour and lord !

That wast not only for thine own

Redeemer—not of these alone

But all to whom thy word was known.

7.

Ten years have wrought their will with me

Since last my words took wing for thee

Who then wast even as now above

Me, and my love.

As then thou knewest not scorn, so now

With that beloved benignant brow

Take these of him whose light wast thou.

FOR A PORTRAIT OF FELICE ORSINI

FOR A PORTRAIT OF FELICE ORSINI.

Steadfast as sorrow, fiery sad, and sweet
    With underthoughts of love and faith, more strong
    Than doubt and hate and all ill thoughts which throng,
Haply, round hope's or fear's world-wandering feet
That find no rest from wandering till they meet
    Death, bearing palms in hand and crowns of song;
    His face, who thought to vanquish wrong with wrong,
Erring, and make rage and redemption meet,
Havoc and freedom; weaving in one weft
Good with his right hand, evil with his left;

But all a hero lived and erred and died;

Looked thus upon the living world he left

So bravely that with pity less than pride

Men hail him Patriot and Tyrannicide.

EVENING ON THE BROADS

EVENING ON THE BROADS.

Over two shadowless waters, adrift as a pinnace in peril,
   Hangs as in heavy suspense, charged with irresolute light,
Softly the soul of the sunset upholden awhile on the sterile
   Waves and wastes of the land, half repossessed by the night.
Inland glimmer the shallows asleep and afar in the breathless
   Twilight: yonder the depths darken afar and asleep.
Slowly the semblance of death out of heaven descends on the deathless
   Waters: hardly the light lives on the face of the deep—

Hardly, but here for awhile. All over the grey soft shallow
  Hover the colours and clouds of the twilight, void of a star.
As a bird unfledged is the broad-winged night, whose winglets are callow
  Yet, but soon with their plumes will she cover her brood from afar,
Cover the brood of her worlds that cumber the skies with their blossom
  Thick as the darkness of leaf-shadowed spring is encumbered with flowers.
World upon world is enwound in the bountiful girth of her bosom,
  Warm and lustrous with life lovely to look on as ours.

EVENING ON THE BROADS.

Still is the sunset adrift as a spirit in doubt that dissembles
    Still with itself, being sick of division and dimmed by dismay—
Nay, not so; but with love and delight beyond passion it trembles,
    Fearful and fain of the night, lovely with love of the day:
Fain and fearful of rest that is like unto death, and begotten
    Out of the womb of the tomb, born of the seed of the grave:
Lovely with shadows of loves that are only not wholly forgotten,
    Only not wholly suppressed by the dark as a wreck by the wave.

Still there linger the loves of the morning and noon, in a vision
   Blindly beheld, but in vain : ghosts that are tired, and would rest.
But the glories beloved of the night rise all too dense for division,
   Deep in the depth of her breast sheltered as doves in a nest.
Fainter the beams of the loves of the daylight season enkindled
   Wane, and the memories of hours that were fair with the love of them fade :
Loftier, aloft of the lights of the sunset stricken and dwindled,
   Gather the signs of the love at the heart of the night new-made.

EVENING ON THE BROADS.

New-made night, new-born of the sunset, immeasurable,
    endless,
  Opens the secret of love hid from of old in her heart,
In the deep sweet heart full-charged with faultless love of
    the friendless
  Spirits of men that are eased when the wheels of the
    sun depart.
Still is the sunset afloat as a ship on the waters upholden
  Full-sailed, wide-winged, poised softly for ever asway—
Nay, not so, but at least for a little, awhile at the golden
  Limit of arching air fain for an hour to delay.
Here on the bar of the sand-bank, steep yet aslope to
    the gleaming
  Waste of the water without, waste of the water within,
Lights overhead and lights underneath seem doubtfully
    dreaming
  Whether the day be done, whether the night may begin.

Far and afar and farther again they falter and hover,
  Warm on the water and deep in the sky and pale on the cloud:
Colder again and slowly remoter, afraid to recover
  Breath, yet fain to revive, as it seems, from the skirt of the shroud.
Faintly the heartbeats shorten and pause of the light in the westward
  Heaven, as eastward quicken the paces of star upon star
Hurried and eager of life as a child that strains to the breast-ward
  Eagerly, yearning forth of the deeps where the ways of them are,
Glad of the glory of the gift of their life and the wealth of its wonder,
  Fain of the night and the sea and the sweet wan face of the earth.

Over them air grows deeper, intense with delight in them :
under
  Things are thrilled in their sleep as with sense of a sure
new birth.
But here by the sand-bank watching, with eyes on the
sea-line, stranger
  Grows to me also the weight of the sea-ridge gazed on
of me,
Heavily heaped up, changefully changeless, void though
of danger
  Void not of menace, but full of the might of the dense
dull sea.
Like as the wave is before me, behind is the bank deep-
drifted ;
  Yellow and thick as the bank is behind me in front is
the wave.

As the wall of a prison imprisoning the mere is the girth of it lifted :
But the rampire of water in front is erect as the wall of a grave.
And the crests of it crumble and topple and change, but the wall is not broken :
Standing still dry-shod, I see it as higher than my head,
Moving inland alway again, reared up as in token
Still of impending wrath still in the foam of it shed.
And even in the pauses between them, dividing the rollers in sunder,
High overhead seems ever the sea-line fixed as a mark,
And the shore where I stand as a valley beholden of hills whence thunder

Cloud and torrent and storm, darkening the depths of the dark.

Up to the sea, not upon it or over it, upward from under
Seems he to gaze, whose eyes yearn after it here from the shore :

A wall of turbid water, aslope to the wide sky's wonder
Of colour and cloud, it climbs, or spreads as a slanted floor.

And the large lights change on the face of the mere like things that were living,
Winged and wonderful, beams like as birds are that pass and are free :

But the light is dense as darkness, a gift withheld in the giving,
That lies as dead on the fierce dull face of the landward sea.

Stained and stifled and soiled, made earthier than earth is and duller,
  Grimly she puts back light as rejected, a thing put away:
No transparent rapture, a molten music of colour;
  No translucent love taken and given of the day.
Fettered and marred and begrimed is the light's live self on her falling,
  As the light of a man's life lighted the fume of a dungeon mars:
Only she knows of the wind, when her wrath gives ear to him calling;
  The delight of the light she knows not, nor answers the sun or the stars.
Love she hath none to return for the luminous love of their giving:
  None to reflect from the bitter and shallow response of her heart

EVENING ON THE BROADS.

Yearly she feeds on her dead, yet herself seems dead and not living,
  Or confused as a soul heavy-laden with trouble that will not depart.
In the sound of her speech to the darkness the moan of her evil remorse is,
  Haply, for strong ships gnawed by the dog-toothed sea-bank's fang
And trampled to death by the rage of the feet of her foam-lipped horses
  Whose manes are yellow as plague, and as ensigns of pestilence hang,
That wave in the foul faint air of the breath of a death-stricken city;
  So menacing heaves she the manes of her rollers knotted with sand,

Discoloured, opaque, suspended in sign as of strength without pity,
That shake with flameless thunder the low long length of the strand.
Here, far off in the farther extreme of the shore as it lengthens
Northward, lonely for miles, ere ever a village begin,
On the lapsing land that recedes as the growth of the strong sea strengthens
Shoreward, thrusting further and further its outworks in,
Here in Shakespeare's vision, a flower of her kin forsaken,
Lay in her golden raiment alone on the wild wave's edge,
Surely by no shore else, but here on the bank storm-shaken,
Perdita, bright as a dew-drop engilt of the sun on the sedge.

EVENING ON THE BROADS.

Here on a shore unbeheld of his eyes in a dream he beheld her
   Outcast, fair as a fairy, the child of a far-off king:
And over the babe-flower gently the head of a pastoral elder
   Bowed, compassionate, hoar as the hawthorn-blossom in spring,
And kind as harvest in autumn: a shelter of shade on the lonely
   Shelterless unknown shore scourged of implacable waves:
Here, where the wind walks royal, alone in his kingdom, and only
   Sounds to the sedges a wail as of triumph that conquers and craves.
All these waters and wastes are his empire of old, and awaken

From barren and stagnant slumber at only the sound
   of his breath :
Yet the hunger is eased not that aches in his heart, nor
   the goal overtaken
  That his wide wings yearn for and labour as hearts that
   yearn after death.
All the solitude sighs and expects with a blind expec-
   tation
  Somewhat unknown of its own sad heart, grown heart-
   sick of strife :
Till sometime its wild heart maddens, and moans, and
   the vast ululation
  Takes wing with the clouds on the waters, and wails to
   be quit of its life.
For the spirit and soul of the waste is the wind, and his
   wings with their waving
  Darken and lighten the darkness and light of it
   thickened or thinned ;

But the heart that impels them is even as a conqueror's insatiably craving
   That victory can fill not, as power cannot satiate the want of the wind.
All these moorlands and marshes are full of his might, and oppose not
   Aught of defence nor of barrier, of forest or precipice piled :
But the will of the wind works ever as his that desires what he knows not,
   And the wail of his want unfulfilled is as one making moan for her child.
And the cry of his triumph is even as the crying of hunger that maddens
   The heart of a strong man aching in vain as the wind's heart aches

And the sadness itself of the land for its infinite solitude saddens
  More for the sound than the silence athirst for the sound that slakes.
And the sunset at last and the twilight are dead: and the darkness is breathless
  With fear of the wind's breath rising that seems and seems not to sleep:
But a sense of the sound of it alway, a spirit unsleeping and deathless,
  Ghost or God, evermore moves on the face of the deep.

THE EMPEROR'S PROGRESS

THE EMPEROR'S PROGRESS.

A STUDY IN THREE STAGES.

(On the Busts of Nero in the Uffizj.)

I.

A CHILD of brighter than the morning's birth
    And lovelier than all smiles that may be smiled
    Save only of little children undefiled,
Sweet, perfect, witless of their own dear worth,
Live rose of love, mute melody of mirth,
    Glad as a bird is when the woods are mild,
    Adorable as is nothing save a child,
Hails with wide eyes and lips his life on earth,

His lovely life with all its heaven to be.

    And whoso reads the name inscribed or hears

    Feels his own heart a frozen well of tears,

Child, for deep dread and fearful pity of thee

Whom God would not let rather die than see

    The incumbent horror of impending years.

II.

Man, that wast godlike being a child, and now,

    No less than kinglike, art no more in sooth

    For all thy grace and lordliness of youth,

The crown that bids men's branded foreheads bow

Much more has branded and bowed down thy brow

    And gnawn upon it as with fire or tooth

    Of steel or snake so sorely, that the truth

Seems here to bear false witness. Is it thou,

Child? and is all the summer of all thy spring
 This? are the smiles that drew men's kisses down
 All faded and transfigured to the frown
That grieves thy face? Art thou this weary thing?
 Then is no slave's load heavier than a crown
And such a thrall no bondman as a king.

III.

Misery, beyond all men's most miserable,
 Absolute, whole, defiant of defence,
 Inevitable, inexplacable, intense,
More vast than heaven is high, more deep than hell,
Past cure or charm of solace or of spell,
 Possesses and pervades the spirit and sense
 Whereto the expanse of the earth pays tribute; whence
Breeds evil only, and broods on fumes that swell

Rank from the blood of brother and mother and wife.
 'Misery of miseries, all is misery,' saith
The heavy fair-faced hateful head, at strife
 With its own lusts that burn with feverous breath
Lips which the loathsome bitterness of life
 Leaves fearful of the bitterness of death.

THE RESURRECTION OF ALCILIA

THE RESURRECTION OF ALCILIA.

(Gratefully inscribed to Dr. A. B. Grosart.)

Sweet song-flower of the Mayspring of our song,

   Be welcome to us, with loving thanks and praise

   To his good hand who travelling on strange ways

Found thee forlorn and fragrant, lain along

Beneath dead leaves that many a winter's wrong

   Had rained and heaped through nigh three centuries' maze

   Above thy Maybloom, hiding from our gaze

The life that in thy leaves lay sweet and strong.

For thine have life, while many above thine head

Piled by the wind lie blossomless and dead.

So now disburdened of such load above
That lay as death's own dust upon thee shed
By days too deaf to hear thee like a dove
Murmuring, we hear thee, bird and flower of love.

THE FOURTEENTH OF JULY

THE FOURTEENTH OF JULY.

(On the refusal by the French Senate of the plenary amnesty demanded by Victor Hugo, in his speech of July 3rd, for the surviving exiles of the Commune.)

Thou shouldst have risen as never dawn yet rose,
    Day of the sunrise of the soul of France,
    Dawn of the whole world's morning, when the trance
Of all the world had end, and all its woes
Respite, prophetic of their perfect close.
    Light of all tribes of men, all names and clans,
    Dawn of the whole world's morning and of man's
Flower of the heart of morning's mystic rose,

Dawn of the very dawn of very day,
  When the sun brighter breaks night's ruinous prison,
  Thou shouldst have risen as yet no dawn has risen,
Evoked of him whose word puts night away,
  Our father, at the music of whose word
  Exile had ended, and the world had heard.

July 5, 1880.

LAUNCH OF THE LIVADIA

Malâ soluta navis exit alite.

                                  HOR.

Rigged with curses dark.

                                  MILTON.

THE LAUNCH OF THE LIVADIA.

I.

Gold, and fair marbles, and again more gold,
    And space of halls afloat that glance and gleam
    Like the green heights of sunset heaven, or seem
The golden steeps of sunrise red and cold
On deserts where dark exile keeps the fold
    Fast of the flocks of torment, where no beam
    Falls of kind light or comfort save in dream,
These we far off behold not, who behold

The cordage woven of curses, and the decks

    With mortal hate and mortal peril paven ;

    From stem to stern the lines of doom engraven

That mark for sure inevitable wrecks

Those sails predestinate, though no storm vex,

    To miss on earth and find in hell their haven.

II.

All curses be about her, and all ill

    Go with her ; heaven be dark above her way,

    The gulf beneath her glad and sure of prey,

And, wheresoe'er her prow be pointed, still

The winds of heaven have all one evil will

    Conspirant even as hearts of kings to slay

    With mouths of kings to lie and smile and pray,

And chiefliest his whose wintrier breath makes chill

With more than winter's and more poisonous cold

    The horror of his kingdom toward the north,

        The deserts of his kingdom toward the east.

And though death hide not in her direful hold

    Be all stars adverse toward her that come forth

        Nightly, by day all hours till all have ceased :

III.

Till all have ceased for ever, and the sum

    Be summed of all the sumless curses told

        Out on his head by all dark seasons rolled

Over its cursed and crowned existence, dumb

And blind and stark as though the snows made numb

    All sense within it, and all conscience cold,

        That hangs round hearts of less imperial mould

Like a snake feeding till their doomsday come.

O heart fast bound of frozen poison, be
All nature's as all true men's hearts to thee,
   A two-edged sword of judgment ; hope be far
And fear at hand for pilot oversea
   With death for compass and despair for star,
   And the white foam a shroud for the White Czar.

September 30, 1880.

SIX YEARS OLD

L

SIX YEARS OLD.

To H. W. M.

Between the springs of six and seven,
   Two fresh years' fountains, clear
Of all but golden sand for leaven,
   Child, midway passing here,
As earth for love's sake dares bless heaven,
   So dare I bless you, dear.

Between two bright well-heads, that brighten
   With every breath that blows
Too loud to lull, too low to frighten,
   But fain to rock, the rose,

Your feet stand fast, your lit smiles lighten,
    That might rear flowers from snows.

You came when winds unleashed were snarling
    Behind the frost-bound hours,
A snow-bird sturdier than the starling,
    A storm-bird fledged for showers,
That spring might smile to find you, darling,
    First born of all the flowers.

Could love make worthy things of worthless,
    My song were worth an ear:
Its note should make the days most mirthless
    The merriest of the year,
And wake to birth all buds yet birthless
    To keep your birthday, dear.

SIX YEARS OLD.

But where your birthday brightens heaven
    No need has earth, God knows,
Of light or warmth to melt or leaven
    The frost or fog that glows
With sevenfold heavenly lights of seven
    Sweet springs that cleave the snows.

Could love make worthy music of you,
    And match my Master's powers,
Had even my loveless heart to love you,
    A better song were ours;
With all the rhymes like stars above you,
    And all the words like flowers.

September 30, 18 0.

A PARTING SONG

A PARTING SONG.

(To a friend leaving England for a year's residence in Australia.)

THESE winds and suns of spring

That warm with breath and wing

The trembling sleep of earth, till half awake

She laughs and blushes ere her slumber break,

For all good gifts they bring

Require one better thing,

For all the loans of joy they lend us, borrow

One sharper dole of sorrow,

To sunder soon by half a world of sea

Her son from England and my friend from me.

Nor hope nor love nor fear

May speed or stay one year,

Nor song nor prayer may bid, as mine would fain,

The seasons perish and be born again,

Restoring all we lend,

Reluctant, of a friend,

The voice, the hand, the presence and the sight

That lend their life and light

To present gladness and heart-strengthening cheer,

Now lent again for one reluctant year.

So much we lend indeed,

Perforce, by force of need,

So much we must ; even these things and no more

The far sea sundering and the sundered shore

A world apart from ours,

So much the imperious hours,

Exact, and spare not ; but no more than these

All earth and all her seas

From thought and faith of trust and truth can borrow,

Not memory from desire, nor hope from sorrow.

  Through bright and dark and bright

  Returns of day and night

I bid the swift year speed and change and give

His breath of life to make the next year live

  With sunnier suns for us

  A life more prosperous,

And laugh with flowers more fragrant, that shall see

A merrier March for me,

A rosier-girdled race of night with day,

A goodlier April and a tenderer May.

        For him the inverted year

        Shall mark our seasons here

With alien alternation, and revive

This withered winter, slaying the spring alive

        With darts more sharply drawn

        As nearer draws the dawn

In heaven transfigured over earth transformed

And with our winters warmed

And wasted with our summers, till the beams

Rise on his face that rose on Dante's dreams.

        Till fourfold morning rise

        Of starshine on his eyes,

Dawn of the spheres that brand steep heaven across

At height of night with semblance of a cross

        Whose grace and ghostly glory

        Poured heaven on purgatory

Seeing with their flamelets risen all heaven grow
    glad
For love thereof it had
And lovely joy of loving ; so may these
Make bright with welcome now their southern seas.

    O happy stars, whose mirth
    The saddest soul on earth
That ever soared and sang found strong to bless,
Lightening his life's harsh load of heaviness
    With comfort sown like seed
    In dream though not in deed
On sprinkled wastes of darkling thought divine,
    Let all your lights now shine
With all as glorious gladness on his eyes
For whom indeed and not in dream they rise.

As those great twins of air

Hailed once with oldworld prayer

Of all folk alway faring forth by sea,

So now may these for grace and guidance be,

To guard his sail and bring

Again to brighten spring

The face we look for and the hand we lack

Still, till they light him back,

As welcome as to first discovering eyes

Their light rose ever, soon on his to rise.

As parting now he goes

From snow-time back to snows,

So back to spring from summer may next year

Restore him, and our hearts receive him here,

The best good gift that spring

Had ever grace to bring

A PARTING SONG.

At fortune's happiest hour of star-blest birth

Back to love's homebright earth,

To eyes with eyes that commune, hand with hand,

And the old warm bosom of all our mother-land.

    Earth and sea-wind and sea

    And stars and sunlight be

Alike all prosperous for him, and all hours

Have all one heart, and all that heart as ours.

    All things as good as strange

    Crown all the seasons' change

With changing flower and compensating fruit

From one year's ripening root ;

Till next year bring us, roused at spring's recall,

A heartier flower and goodlier fruit than all.

March 26, 1880.

BY THE NORTH SEA

M

TO WALTER THEODORE WATTS.

'We are what suns and winds and waters make us.'—LANDOR.

SEA, wind, and sun, with light and sound and breath
    The spirit of man fulfilling—these create
    That joy wherewith man's life grown passionate
Gains heart to hear and sense to read and faith
To know the secret word our Mother saith
    In silence, and to see, though doubt wax great,
    Death as the shadow cast by life on fate,
Passing, whose shade we call the shadow of death.

Brother, to whom our Mother as to me
    Is dearer than all dreams of days undone,
This song I give you of the sovereign three
    That are as life and sleep and death are, one:
A song the sea-wind gave me from the sea,
    Where nought of man's endures before the sun.

BY THE NORTH SEA.

I.

1.

A LAND that is lonelier than ruin ;
   A sea that is stranger than death :
Far fields that a rose never blew in,
   Wan waste where the winds lack breath ;
Waste endless and boundless and flowerless
   But of marsh-blossoms fruitless as free :
Where earth lies exhausted, as powerless
   To strive with the sea.

2.

Far flickers the flight of the swallows,
    Far flutters the weft of the grass
Spun dense over desolate hollows
    More pale than the clouds as they pass:
Thick woven as the weft of a witch is
    Round the heart of a thrall that hath sinned,
Whose youth and the wrecks of its riches
    Are waifs on the wind.

3.

The pastures are herdless and sheepless,
    No pasture or shelter for herds:
The wind is relentless and sleepless,
    And restless and songless the birds;

Their cries from afar fall breathless,
    Their wings are as lightnings that flee ;
For the land has two lords that are deathless :
    Death's self, and the sea.

4.

These twain, as a king with his fellow,
    Hold converse of desolate speech :
And her waters are haggard and yellow
    And crass with the scurf of the beach :
And his garments are grey as the hoary
    Wan sky where the day lies dim ;
And his power is to her, and his glory,
    As hers unto him.

5.

In the pride of his power she rejoices,
    In her glory he glows and is glad :

In her darkness the sound of his voice is,

    With his breath she dilates and is mad :

'If thou slay me, O death, and outlive me,

    Yet thy love hath fulfilled me of thee.'

'Shall I give thee not back if thou give me,

    O sister, O sea?'

6.

And year upon year dawns living,

    And age upon age drops dead :

And his hand is not weary of giving,

    And the thirst of her heart is not fed :

And the hunger that moans in her passion,

    And the rage in her hunger that roars,

As a wolf's that the winter lays lash on,

    Still calls and implores.

7.

Her walls have no granite for girder,
    No fortalice fronting her stands :
But reefs the bloodguiltiest of murder
    Are less than the banks of her sands :
These number their slain by the thousand ;
    For the ship hath no surety to be,
When the bank is abreast of her bows and
        Aflush with the sea.

8.

No surety to stand, and no shelter
    To dawn out of darkness but one,
Out of waters that hurtle and welter
    No succour to dawn with the sun

But a rest from the wind as it passes,

    Where, hardly redeemed from the waves,

Lie thick as the blades of the grasses

    The dead in their graves.

9.

A multitude noteless of numbers,

    As wild weeds cast on an heap :

And sounder than sleep are their slumbers,

    And softer than song is their sleep ;

And sweeter than all things and stranger

    The sense, if perchance it may be,

That the wind is divested of danger

    And scatheless the sea.

10.

That the roar of the banks they breasted

    Is hurtless as bellowing of herds,

And the strength of his wings that invested
   The wind, as the strength of a bird's ;
As the sea-mew's might or the swallow's
   That cry to him back if he cries,
As over the graves and their hollows
     Days darken and rise.

II.

As the souls of the dead men disburdened
   And clean of the sins that they sinned,
With a lovelier than man's life guerdoned
   And delight as a wave's in the wind,
And delight as the wind's in the billow,
   Birds pass, and deride with their glee
The flesh that has dust for its pillow
     As wrecks have the sea.

12.

When the ways of the sun wax dimmer,
 Wings flash through the dusk like beams;
As the clouds in the lit sky glimmer,
 The bird in the graveyard gleams;
As the cloud at its wing's edge whitens
 When the clarions of sunrise are heard,
The graves that the bird's note brightens
 Grow bright for the bird.

13.

As the waves of the numberless waters
 That the wind cannot number who guides
Are the sons of the shore and the daughters
 Here lulled by the chime of the tides:

And here in the press of them standing

   We know not if these or if we

Live truliest, or anchored to landing

      Or drifted to sea.

14.

In the valley he named of decision

   No denser were multitudes met

When the soul of the seer in her vision

   Saw nations for doom of them set;

Saw darkness in dawn, and the splendour

   Of judgment, the sword and the rod;

But the doom here of death is more tender

      And gentler the god.

15.

And gentler the wind from the dreary
    Sea-banks by the waves overlapped,
Being weary, speaks peace to the weary
    From slopes that the tide-stream hath sapped;
And sweeter than all that we call so
    The seal of their slumber shall be
Till the graves that embosom them also
    Be sapped of the sea.

II.

1.

For the heart of the waters is cruel,
   And the kisses are dire of their lips,
And their waves are as fire is to fuel
   To the strength of the sea-faring ships,
Though the sea's eye gleam as a jewel
   To the sun's eye back as he dips.

2.

Though the sun's eye flash to the sea's
   Live light of delight and of laughter,

And her lips breathe back to the breeze
  The kiss that the wind's lips waft her
From the sun that subsides, and sees
  No gleam of the storm's dawn after.

3.

And the wastes of the wild sea-marches
  Where the borderers are matched in their might—
Bleak fens that the sun's weight parches,
  Dense waves that reject his light—
Change under the change-coloured arches
  Of changeless morning and night.

4.

The waves are as ranks enrolled
  Too close for the storm to sever:

BY THE NORTH SEA.

The fens lie naked and cold,
   But their heart fails utterly never :
The lists are set from of old,
   And the warfare endureth for ever.

III

I

Miles, and miles, and miles of desolation!
    Leagues on leagues on leagues without a change!
Sign or token of some eldest nation
    Here would make the strange land not so strange.
Time-forgotten, yea since time's creation,
    Seem these borders where the sea-birds range.

2.

Slowly, gladly, full of peace and wonder
    Grows his heart who journeys here alone.
Earth and all its thoughts of earth sink under
    Deep as deep in water sinks a stone.
Hardly knows it if the rollers thunder,
    Hardly whence the lonely wind is blown.

3.

Tall the plumage of the rush-flower tosses,
    Sharp and soft in many a curve and line
Gleam and glow the sea-coloured marsh-mosses,
    Salt and splendid from the circling brine.
Streak on streak of glimmering seashine crosses
    All the land sea-saturate as with wine.

4.

Far, and far between, in divers orders,
  Clear grey steeples cleave the low grey sky;
Fast and firm as time-unshaken warders,
  Hearts made sure by faith, by hope made high.
These alone in all the wild sea-borders
  Fear no blast of days and nights that die.

5.

All the land is like as one man's face is,
  Pale and troubled still with change of cares.
Doubt and death pervade her clouded spaces:
  Strength and length of life and peace are theirs;
Theirs alone amid these weary places,
  Seeing not how the wild world frets and fares.

6.

Firm and fast where all is cloud that changes
  Cloud-clogged sunlight, cloud by sunlight thinned,
Stern and sweet, above the sand-hill ranges
  Watch the towers and tombs of men that sinned
Once, now calm as earth whose only change is
  Wind, and light, and wind, and cloud, and wind.

7.

Out and in and out the sharp straits wander,
  In and out and in the wild way strives,
Starred and paved and lined with flowers that squander
  Gold as golden as the gold of hives,
Salt and moist and multiform: but yonder,
  See, what sign of life or death survives?

8.

Seen then only when the songs of olden
  Harps were young whose echoes yet endure,
Hymned of Homer when his years were golden,
  Known of only when the world was pure,
Here is Hades, manifest, beholden,
  Surely, surely here, if aught be sure!

9.

Where the border-line was crossed, that, sundering
  Death from life, keeps weariness from rest,
None can tell, who fares here forward wondering;
  None may doubt but here might end his quest.
Here life's lightning joys and woes once thundering
  Sea-like round him cease like storm suppressed.

10.

Here the wise wave-wandering steadfast-hearted
    Guest of many a lord of many a land
Saw the shape or shade of years departed,
    Saw the semblance risen and hard at hand,
Saw the mother long from love's reach parted,
    Anticleia, like a statue stand.

11.

Statue? nay, nor tissued image woven
    Fair on hangings in his father's hall;
Nay, too fast her faith of heart was proven,
    Far too firm her loveliest love of all;
Love wherethrough the loving heart was cloven,
    Love that hears not when the loud Fates call.

12.

Love that lives and stands up re-created
    Then when life has ebbed and anguish fled;
Love more strong than death or all things fated,
    Child's and mother's, lit by love and led;
Love that found what life so long awaited
    Here, when life came down among the dead.

13.

Here, where never came alive another,
    Came her son across the sundering tide
Crossed before by many a warrior brother
    Once that warred on Ilion at his side;
Here spread forth vain hands to clasp the mother
    Dead, that sorrowing for his love's sake died.

14.

Parted, though by narrowest of divisions,
  Clasp he might not, only might implore,
Sundered yet by bitterest of derisions,
  Son, and mother from the son she bore—
Here? But all dispeopled here of visions
  Lies, forlorn of shadows even, the shore.

15.

All too sweet such men's Hellenic speech is,
  All too fain they lived of light to see,
Once to see the darkness of these beaches,
  Once to sing this Hades found of me
Ghostless, all its gulfs and creeks and reaches,
  Sky, and shore, and cloud, and waste, and sea.

IV.

1.

But aloft and afront of me faring

    Far forward as folk in a dream

That strive, between doubting and daring

    Right on till the goal for them gleam,

Full forth till their goal on them lighten,

    The harbour where fain they would be,

What headlands there darken and brighten?

    What change in the sea?

2.

What houses and woodlands that nestle

   Safe inland to lee of the hill

As it slopes from the headlands that wrestle

   And succumb to the strong sea's will?

Truce is not, nor respite, nor pity,

   For the battle is waged not of hands

Where over the grave of a city

   The ghost of it stands.

3.

Where the wings of the sea-wind slacken,

   Green lawns to the landward thrive,

Fields brighten and pine-woods blacken,

   And the heat in their heart is alive;

They blossom and warble and murmur,
　For the sense of their spirit is free :
But harder to shoreward and firmer
　The grasp of the sea.

4.

Like ashes the low cliffs crumble,
　The banks drop down into dust,
The heights of the hills are made humble,
　As a reed's is the strength of their trust :
As a city's that armies environ,
　The strength of their stay is of sand :
But the grasp of the sea is as iron,
　Laid hard on the land.

5.

A land that is thirstier than ruin ;
　A sea that is hungrier than death ;
Heaped hills that a tree never grew in ;
　Wide sands where the wave draws breath ;
All solace is here for the spirit
　That ever for ever may be
For the soul of thy son to inherit,
　　My mother, my sea.

6.

O delight of the headlands and beaches !
　O desire of the wind on the wold,
More glad than a man's when it reaches
　That end which it sought from of old

And the palm of possession is dreary
   To the sense that in search of it sinned;
But nor satisfied ever nor weary
   Is ever the wind.

7.

The delight that he takes but in living
   Is more than of all things that live:
For the world that has all things for giving
   Has nothing so goodly to give:
But more than delight his desire is,
   For the goal where his pinions would be
Is immortal as air or as fire is,
   Immense as the sea.

8.

Though hence come the moan that he borrows
    From darkness and depth of the night,
Though hence be the spring of his sorrows,
    Hence too is the joy of his might;
The delight that his doom is for ever
    To seek and desire and rejoice,
And the sense that eternity never
    Shall silence his voice.

9.

That satiety never may stifle
    Nor weariness ever estrange
Nor time be so strong as to rifle
    Nor change be so great as to change

His gift that renews in the giving,
   The joy that exalts him to be
Alone of all elements living
   The lord of the sea.

10.

What is fire, that its flame should consume her?
   More fierce than all fires are her waves:
What is earth, that its gulfs should entomb her?
   More deep are her own than their graves.
Life shrinks from his pinions that cover
   The darkness by thunders bedinned:
But she knows him, her lord and her lover,
   The godhead of wind.

11.

For a season his wings are about her,
 His breath on her lips for a space;
Such rapture he wins not without her
 In the width of his worldwide race.
Though the forests bow down, and the mountains
 Wax dark, and the tribes of them flee,
His delight is more deep in the fountains
 And springs of the sea.

12.

There are those too of mortals that love him,
 There are souls that desire and require,
Be the glories of midnight above him
 Or beneath him the daysprings of fire:

And their hearts are as harps that approve him
   And praise him as chords of a lyre
That were fain with their music to move him
   To meet their desire.

13.

To descend through the darkness to grace them,
   Till darkness were lovelier than light:
To encompass and grasp and embrace them,
   Till their weakness were one with his might:
With the strength of his wings to caress them,
   With the blast of his breath to set free;
With the mouths of his thunders to bless them
   For sons of the sea.

14.

For these have the toil and the guerdon
    That the wind has eternally : these
Have part in the boon and the burden
    Of the sleepless unsatisfied breeze,
That finds not, but seeking rejoices
    That possession can work him no wrong :
And the voice at the heart of their voice is
    The sense of his song.

15.

For the wind's is their doom and their blessing ;
    To desire, and have always above
A possession beyond their possessing,
    A love beyond reach of their love.

Green earth has her sons and her daughters,
   And these have their guerdons ; but we
Are the wind's and the sun's and the water's,
   Elect of the sea.

V

1

For the sea too seeks and rejoices,
   Gains and loses and gains,
And the joy of her heart's own choice is
   As ours, and as ours are her pains:
As the thoughts of our hearts are her voices,
   And as hers is the pulse of our veins.

2.

Her fields that know not of dearth
   Nor lie for their fruit's sake fallow

Laugh large in the depth of their mirth :

But inshore here in the shallow,

Embroiled with encumbrance of earth,

Their skirts are turbid and yellow.

3.

The grime of her greed is upon her,

The sign of her deed is her soil ;

As the earth's is her own dishonour,

And corruption the crown of her toil :

She hath spoiled and devoured, and her honour

Is this, to be shamed by her spoil.

4.

But afar where pollution is none,

Nor ensign of strife nor endeavour,

Where her heart and the sun's are one,
    And the soil of her sin comes never,
She is pure as the wind and the sun,
    And her sweetness endureth for ever.

VI

1.

Death, and change, and darkness everlasting,
   Deaf, that hears not what the daystar saith,
Blind, past all remembrance and forecasting,
   Dead, past memory that it once drew breath ;
These, above the washing tides and wasting,
   Reign, and rule this land of utter death.

2.

Change of change, darkness of darkness, hidden,
   Very death of very death, begun
When none knows,—the knowledge is forbidden—
   Self-begotten, self-proceeding, one,
Born, not made—abhorred, unchained, unchidden,
   Night stands here defiant of the sun.

3.

Change of change, and death of death begotten,
   Darkness born of darkness, one and three,
Ghostly godhead of a world forgotten,
   Crowned with heaven, enthroned on land and sea,
Here, where earth with dead men's bones is rotten,
   God of Time, thy likeness worships thee.

4.

Lo, thy likeness of thy desolation,
   Shape and figure of thy might, O Lord,
Formless form, incarnate miscreation,
   Served of all things living and abhorred ;
Earth herself is here thine incarnation,
   Time, of all things born on earth adored.

5.

All that worship thee are fearful of thee ;
   No man may not worship thee for fear :
Prayers nor curses prove not nor disprove thee,
   Move nor change thee with our change of cheer :
All at last, though all abhorred thee, love thee,
   God, the sceptre of whose throne is here.

6.

Here thy throne and sceptre of thy station,
  Here the palace paven for thy feet ;
Here thy sign from nation unto nation
  Passed as watchword for thy guards to greet,
Guards that go before thine exaltation,
  Ages, clothed with bitter years and sweet.

7.

Here, where sharp the sea-bird shrills his ditty,
  Flickering flame-wise through the clear live calm,
Rose triumphal, crowning all a city,
  Roofs exalted once with prayer and psalm,
Built of holy hands for holy pity,
  Frank and fruitful as a sheltering palm.

8.

Church and hospice wrought in faultless fashion,
　　Hall and chancel bounteous and sublime,
Wide and sweet and glorious as compassion,
　　Filled and thrilled with force of choral chime,
Filled with spirit of prayer and thrilled with passion
　　Hailed a God more merciful than Time.

9.

Ah, less mighty, less than Time prevailing,
　　Shrunk, expelled, made nothing at his nod,
Less than clouds across the sea-line sailing,
　　Lies he, stricken by his master's rod.
'Where is man?' the cloister murmurs wailing;
　　Back the mute shrine thunders—'Where is God?'

10.

Here is all the end of all his glory—
  Dust, and grass, and barren silent stones.
Dead, like him, one hollow tower and hoary
  Naked in the sea-wind stands and moans,
Filled and thrilled with its perpetual story:
  Here, where earth is dense with dead men's bones.

11.

Low and loud and long, a voice for ever,
  Sounds the wind's clear story like a song.
Tomb from tomb the waves devouring sever,
  Dust from dust as years relapse along;
Graves where men made sure to rest, and never
  Lie dismantled by the seasons' wrong.

12.

Now displaced, devoured and desecrated,
    Now by Time's hands darkly disinterred,
These poor dead that sleeping here awaited
    Long the archangel's re-creating word,
Closed about with roofs and walls high-gated
    Till the blast of judgment should be heard,

13.

Naked, shamed, cast out of consecration,
    Corpse and coffin, yea the very graves,
Scoffed at, scattered, shaken from their station,
    Spurned and scourged of wind and sea like slaves,
Desolate beyond man's desolation,
    Shrink and sink into the waste of waves.

14.

Tombs, with bare white piteous bones protruded,
   Shroudless, down the loose collapsing banks,
Crumble, from their constant place detruded,
   That the sea devours and gives not thanks.
Graves where hope and prayer and sorrow brooded
   Gape and slide and perish, ranks on ranks.

15.

Rows on rows and line by line they crumble,
   They that thought for all time through to be.
Scarce a stone whereon a child might stumble
   Breaks the grim field paced alone of me.
Earth, and man, and all their gods wax humble
   Here, where Time brings pasture to the sea.

VII.

1.

But afar on the headland exalted,
    But beyond in the curl of the bay,
From the depth of his dome deep-vaulted
    Our father is lord of the day.
Our father and lord that we follow,
    For deathless and ageless is he;
And his robe is the whole sky's hollow,
    His sandal the sea.

2.

Where the horn of the headland is sharper,
   And her green floor glitters with fire,
The sea has the sun for a harper,
   The sun has the sea for a lyre.
The waves are a pavement of amber,
   By the feet of the sea-winds trod
To receive in a god's presence-chamber
   Our father, the God.

3.

Time, haggard and changeful and hoary,
   Is master and God of the land:
But the air is fulfilled of the glory
   That is shed from our lord's right hand.

O father of all of us ever,

 All glory be only to thee

From heaven, that is void of thee never,

 And earth, and the sea.

4.

O Sun, whereof all is beholden,

 Behold now the shadow of this death,

This place of the sepulchres, olden

 And emptied and vain as a breath.

The bloom of the bountiful heather

 Laughs broadly beyond in thy light

As dawn, with her glories to gather,

 At darkness and night.

5.

Though the Gods of the night lie rotten
    And their honour be taken away
And the noise of their names forgotten,
    Thou, Lord, art God of the day.
Thou art father and saviour and spirit,
    O Sun, of the soul that is free
And hath grace of thy grace to inherit
    Thine earth and thy sea.

6.

The hills and the sands and the beaches,
    The waters adrift and afar,
The banks and the creeks and the reaches,
    How glad of thee all these are !

The flowers, overflowing, overcrowded,
    Are drunk with the mad wind's mirth :
The delight of thy coming unclouded
    Makes music of earth.

7.

I, last least voice of her voices,
    Give thanks that were mute in me long
To the soul in my soul that rejoices
    For the song that is over my song.
Time gives what he gains for the giving
    Or takes for his tribute of me ;
My dreams to the wind everliving,
    My song to the sea.

Spottiswoode & Co. Printers, New-street Square, London.

www.ingramcontent.com/pod-product-compliance
Lightning Source LLC
Chambersburg PA
CBHW020822230426
43666CB00007B/1056